The Overprivileged, Underqualified Manifesto

by Giovi

Author's Note

This book is for the ones who still show up with integrity. For the brilliant voices buried under bureaucracy. For the souls made small by systems that reward swagger over soul.

There is still hope. There always has been. But only if we name what's broken and refuse to play by the rules of the broken game.

This book is dedicated to my colleagues, my friends who shared with me these tumultuous times, and my dear family who have been my source of hope and my drive to persevere, who have given me love, understanding, and comprehension when I needed them most.

The narratives in this book draw on the author's direct experience
and publicly available sources. To safeguard privacy, names, roles,
and other identifying characteristics may be changed, combined,
or omitted; several scenarios reflect composites that illustrate
recurrent patterns rather than single incidents. When organizations
are referenced, citations are to public reporting where possible;
interpretations and conclusions are the author's alone. This book
offers commentary and analysis for general information; it is
not legal, investment, or employment advice. Any resemblance
to people not expressly identified is coincidental. The views
expressed here do not reflect those of the author's employers,
clients, partners, or any affiliated institutions, past or present.

Edited by Leslie Wilson
Cover Page Art by Susie Williams
Typesetting by Barış Şehri
Set in 12/14,75pt Adobe Garamond Pro

Table of Contents

Foreword

I began writing this book long before I ever put pen to paper, over twenty years ago, when I first stepped into the corporate world through the doors of a major multinational in IT. I didn't plan to write this. It began as an observation, so I waited. I lived. I gave the system the benefit of the doubt. I believed that, eventually, it would correct itself. That merit would rise above maneuvering. That competence would outlast charisma. That, quietly and surely, those who knew how to build would be lifted above those who knew only how to brand. I believed the empire of politics would collapse under the weight of its own absurdity.

But none of it happened.

I watched too many leadership positions be handed not to the brilliant but to the available, the palatable, the well-connected. I watched companies forget their purpose, swallowed by turf wars disguised as strategy. Vision was replaced with vanity. Integrity was sidelined by optics. Meetings became theater. Promotions became transactions. Worst of all, the quiet workers, the capable ones, began to disappear.

Some walked away. Others stayed, but not as themselves.

There is grief, a helpless ache, in watching something you care about decay from the inside. Still, I'm writing this not to despair, but to remember. To hold a mirror up to the madness. To say: We see what's happening. We feel it in our bones. And we are not alone.

Work has always been, and will continue to be, one of the most defining parts of our lives. For many, it's a source of purpose and stability, the engine that gives life meaning and the foundation that provides the security to pursue personal dreams. Whether that means starting a family, exploring the world, embracing new cultures, or building long-term wealth, work is the lever that makes it possible.

But work doesn't come without cost.

More often than not, it arrives with barriers, some visible, many hidden. These challenges can drain more than just your energy. They can chip away at your motivation, your sense of self-worth, and your belief in a better future. And when that erosion builds, it doesn't stay confined to your office or your laptop. It follows you home. It seeps into your relationships. It casts shadows over your most personal spaces.

For a long time, I stayed silent. But silence, I've learned, has a cost. And over time, that cost became unbearable for me. What finally broke me wasn't a single betrayal or a failed project; it was the realization that the rot wasn't an exception. It was the system. That what we were experiencing wasn't a temporary downturn. It was cultural erosion disguised as normalcy.

So, I began to write, not out of bitterness, but out of necessity. To say what too many have been told to swallow. To name what's broken.

THE TRUTH IS THIS Much of our leadership is not equipped to lead. Instead of courage, they rely on control. Instead of vision, they weaponize time and politics, tools made not for progress, but for survival. These unequipped leaders build strategies not to solve problems, but to outlast them. Until every good employee has either burned out, given up, or walked away. And in some cases, by then, there's no company left to save.

After more than two decades immersed in digital transformation, spanning the evolution from procedural to relational databases, from monolithic systems to distributed clusters, from standalone computing to mobile-first communication strategies, I've had the rare privilege of witnessing, living through, and adapting to the tectonic shifts that have shaped the technology landscape. My journey has taken me across continents and cultures, from Latin America to Europe, Mexico to India, Brazil to the United States. Each chapter added a new perspective on how different regions, industries, and leadership styles confront the demands of modernization.

Landing in the financial technology sector in the United States, I began to connect the dots. I realized that despite differences in geography or market maturity, a troubling pattern persists throughout. Most organizational failures in the digital age can be traced not to the complexity of technology itself, but to the poverty of leadership that governs it. A leadership class more focused on optics than outcomes. Leaders who sidestep innovation, resist disruption, and lean instead on political maneuvering and short-term metrics to secure their positions.

This failure isn't just a tactical misstep; it's a strategic collapse. By prioritizing shareholder returns over genuine investment in research and development, cultivating talent, and building resilient, adaptive cultures, these executives are actively mortgaging the future of their industries. The damage is compounded by their entanglement in internal politics, where influence is used not to accelerate progress but to stall it, to delay change until it's too late or too costly to matter.

The consequence? A generation of organizations that move slower than the world around them. Institutions that once led their fields now teeter on irrelevance, their futures mortgaged by visionless stewardship.

What lies ahead demands a different kind of leadership rooted in courage, long-term thinking, and moral clarity. Without a radical realignment of values and priorities, many of today's most recognizable institutions will not just falter; they will vanish, and with them, the credibility and influence they once held in shaping the global economy.

Introduction

Too many executives now measure their success not by the resilience of their institutions, but by the preservation of their roles. They speak of innovation while smothering it. They reward loyalty, not learning. They chase quarterly highs while mortgaging for long-term health. And in the process, they leave behind cultures that are cynical, brittle, and slow.

The consequences of this misalignment are already upon us. Organizations that once defined their fields are now stumbling into obsolescence. Customers are drifting. Talent is burning out. Trust, once a quiet strength, is cracking under the weight of performance theater.

What lies ahead will not wait. The future demands something more than polished rhetoric or half-hearted pilots. It demands leaders who are willing to be uncomfortable. To be wrong. To grow. To center mission over ego, and substance over spin.

Without a radical recalibration of how we define and reward leadership, many of today's most powerful institutions will not survive the decade, not because they lack money or market share, but because they've lost their soul.

This book is for those who refuse to look away. For those still trying, still building, still hoping. For those who believe transformation is still possible, if we stop lying to ourselves about what's standing in the way.

The Perils of Political Gamesmanship

Adding to the inertia is a disturbing trend of politicized decision-making. Managers and executives of corporations have increasingly intertwined themselves with personal political agendas, often wielding influence in shaping processes and procedures that prioritize their own interest and comfort over innovation, equity, culture, and environmental responsibility.

A pervasive issue within many organizations is the insidious practice of political maneuvering. Managers often prioritize personal gain and the maintenance of the status quo over strategic decision-making and long-term organizational health. This political entanglement can lead to a host of negative consequences, including:

Stagnation and inertia: Political infighting can stifle innovation and progress. Managers may prioritize maintaining their power base over taking risks or challenging the status quo.

Dysfunctional decision-making: Decisions are often made based on political considerations rather than merit, leading to suboptimal outcomes.

Eroded trust and morale: A toxic political environment can erode trust among employees, leading to decreased morale, productivity, and retention.

Ethical compromises: In their pursuit of power, some managers may resort to unethical tactics, such as backstabbing, rumormongering, and scapegoating.

In many industries, the influence of corporate politics is particularly pronounced. For instance, in the technology sector, executives may prioritize short-term gains, such as stock price increases over long-term investments in research and development. This can lead to a decline in innovation and a loss of competitive advantage.

Similarly, in the healthcare industry, political maneuvering can impede efforts to improve patient care and reduce costs. For example, pharmaceutical companies may lobby for policies that protect their profits, even if these policies harm patients.

Consequences on Workforce and Society

The repercussions of these failures are far-reaching. At the workforce level, employees suffer under stagnant leadership that fails to equip them with the tools and training necessary to thrive in a changing technological landscape. Instead of fostering a culture of experimentation and learning, many corporations slash budgets for employee development and innovation in favor of short-term profitability metrics. This has created a generation of workers who are underprepared for the jobs of tomorrow.

On a societal level, the reluctance to adapt to technological trends, like AI, green tech, and digital transformation, exacerbates inequality and erodes consumer trust. The United States, for example, risks falling behind global competitors like China and the EU. Though the United States is a cradle of innovation, these other regions are jumping ahead when it comes to adopting innovation and embedding it into a real, cohesive culture. They're also actively accelerating innovation through coordinated public-private initiatives and regulatory foresight, while American institutions remain hampered by inertia, short-termism, and fragmented governance.

Chapter 1: The Mirage of Digital Transformation

The Illusion of Progress

I'll never forget the first slide.

A full-team meeting had been called, and fifty-four of us sat crammed into a conference room meant for forty. We were engineers, analysts, project managers, veterans of the tech world, many with over a decade of experience building complex systems, solving real problems, and delivering tangible results. This meeting was special, we were told. It would serve as a kickoff to a new digital transformation initiative that would modernize our operations, redefine our purpose, and position us for the future. Or so we hoped.

The projector flickered to life. "Welcome to Fisher University."

Below that title slide, centered and glowing with misplaced corporate pride, was a pixelated photo of our VP, Karen Fisher, during her college years: shoulder pads, big hair, and a grainy relic more suited to a social media throwback than a professional unveiling.

The silence that filled the room was not respectful anticipation; it was cautious skepticism. I remember clearly the sideways glances exchanged between colleagues, the quiet sighs and half-hidden smirks. We had seen disappointing presentations before, but something about this one was uniquely unsettling.

Our VP stood proudly next to the screen, smiling as if accepting a lifetime achievement award rather than starting a major initiative. Her opening words were confident and rehearsed: "I am a specialist, not a generalist." The statement hung in the air and was meant to be impressive, but to anyone listening closely, it revealed emptiness. Because what followed was neither a vision nor a strategy; it wasn't even an acknowledgment of our real challenges. It was a brazen admission, delivered without hesitation or humility, that she did not understand the technical or business mechanics of our industry's core product: financial transactions.

Even more startlingly, we considered her admission to be a declaration that she didn't need to know. Her authority, she proudly explained, was not derived from expertise or technical understanding or clear vision. It came from her pay grade, earned not through innovation or proven outcomes, but through fifteen years of navigating corporate politics, surviving the system, and befriending the right executives.

And then she said it outright, what most people whispered cautiously in hallways or during private chats. Eighty percent of her speech revolved around one single message: Careers in this company were built not on solving problems or delivering results, but on securing sponsorship from senior executives. This, she proclaimed, was the real curriculum of Fisher University. Here, success hinged on proximity to power, on mastering internal relationships rather than navigating production outages or executing critical migrations.

In that instant, whatever fragile hope we had held that this initiative might genuinely transform in a meaningful way, collapsed. The message was painfully clear: This wasn't transformation. It was performance. We weren't asked to innovate. We were asked to perform loyalty.

And perform we did. Polite applause followed, punctuated by obligatory compliments, the kind uttered not because they were genuine but because every single one of us had something valuable to protect. We had mortgages, immigration visas, and families depending on the next paycheck. Staying silent was a necessary protection when the only alternative was risking retaliation, or worse, being labeled as "difficult" or "not a team player."

Yet, as I glanced around, I felt a deeper sadness beyond mere disappointment. It wasn't the absurdity of the VP's presentation; many of us had endured worse. It was the quiet dignity of the people in that room that struck me— more than fifty souls, each carrying stories of long nights, impossible deadlines, second chances, and first-generation dreams. Engineers who had reinvented themselves in foreign lands, analysts who studied late into the night after their children had fallen asleep, architects who built expertise brick by brick rather than having it handed to them by lineage or lunch meetings with executives.

These weren't just employees. They were quiet warriors, living far from homes they still missed deeply, speaking second languages fluently but never without effort, working twice as hard to prove they belonged. And yet, there we sat, clapping for someone whose career trajectory had been carried by a current of entitlement rather than earned skill.

We clapped not out of respect, but out of fear, fear of the subtle retaliation that follows even mild dissent, fear of losing the fragile equilibrium that kept our personal world stable. Beneath the applause, resentment simmered. Not envy, but resentment born from injustice. We were watching something sacred, skill, ambition, sacrifice, be cheapened by someone whose only real risk had been choosing the right people at the right dinner party.

Moments like these don't simply demoralize; they hollow you out. They make you question whether your skill, your effort, and your integrity even matter in a place where power is inherited, not earned. No matter if the tools are introduced, the frameworks adopted, or the jargon splashed across PowerPoint slides, transformation is impossible if leadership places themselves over the mission. A culture rewarding loyalty over capability only dresses dysfunction in pretty clothes.

Symptoms of Failure

The Fisher University kickoff wasn't unique; it was merely a particularly vivid performance of a script I had seen repeatedly countless times. Different companies, different leaders, across continents and cultures, all share the same pattern: technology treated as a costume rather than a catalyst.

I've watched multimillion-dollar programs collapse under their own dishonesty. Grand announcements followed by hurried implementations. Agile methods proclaimed boldly, only to expose the same old waterfall habits disguised within short sprints. Cloud migrations announced triumphantly yet limited to superficial lift-and-shifts, because nobody dared question the deeper architecture, lest they disturb powerful owners of outdated systems. Data strategies championed by leaders who struggled to interpret a basic dashboard without their assistants.

The symptoms are unmistakable. Leaders obsess over metrics, delivery speed, and feature counts, ignoring whether these features actually solve problems or deliver real value or are part of a long-term vision. Endless workshops and town halls pretend to engage employees, but decisions are premade behind closed doors. Pilot projects designed for press releases never scale, never integrate, and never truly challenge the status quo.

Then comes the churn, the quiet exodus of good people. Not because they can't do the job, but because they refuse to keep pretending that their jobs match the leadership's lofty claims. Engineers once passionately outspoken retreat into silence. Designers once confident enough to challenge assumptions simply nod, resigned. Teams capable of incredible creativity dissolve into confusion and cautious compliance. The message becomes clear: Don't push too hard, don't question too deeply, and never outshine the wrong leader.

Yet, amidst this dysfunction, executives continue hiding behind empty slogans:

"We're in this together."

"This is your second home."

"We're one family."

I've heard these platitudes from leaders who spend most of their time in meetings behind closed doors, surrounded by loyal lieutenants who made careers out of constant agreement. These leaders dismiss alarming survey results, write off declining morale as "chemistry issues," and hire corporate psychologists to redirect attention away from their failures.

We've all been urged to share our honest feelings in those carefully staged "feedback" meetings, only to have truths reframed as negativity or discontent by the people hired not to diagnose the system's dysfunction, but to medicate its symptoms and guide conversations away from leadership and toward personalities.

Real Teams

Real teams aren't built through staged outings or slogans about "family." They don't come to life because someone mandated fun. They come from something deeper—something earned, not given.

Trust, the kind that transforms a group of colleagues into a true team, emerges from shared struggle. From nights when deadlines loomed and someone stayed late without being asked. From the quiet intensity of knowing your teammate is watching your blind spot, not for credit, but because they care. It comes from genuine debate, where people can disagree honestly and challenge each other respectfully without fear of political backlash.

It grows in collective respect, not respect handed down by title or tenure, but respect earned through grit, competence, and integrity.

It's sealed in real achievement, not the kind on a dashboard, but the kind you feel when a broken system is finally rebuilt, when the impossible becomes reality because of a team that refused to break.

And maybe most of all, it's born in recovery, from failure, from missteps, from near-collapse. When something goes wrong, no one points fingers. People step forward, take ownership, and lift each other up. That's where trust solidifies, not in perfection, but in repair.

I know this because I've lived it.

I've been part of those teams. Teams that leave a mark far deeper than a project milestone or a LinkedIn endorsement. A kind of brotherhood, a kind of sisterhood, that lasts beyond roles, companies, and even careers. Years later, on different continents, in different jobs, we still check in. We still root for each other. Because we remember who we were when we stood together. And we know, collectively, we were powerful.

No workshop can replicate that. No slogan can shortcut it. That kind of connection is earned. And it is the only soil in which true transformation can take root.

The Cost of Comfort

It's tempting to dismiss a bad meeting, tone-deaf leadership, or delayed projects as isolated mistakes on a long journey toward progress. But these aren't just symptoms; they're entrenched patterns, compounding and repeating, defining the very culture of an organization.

I've witnessed organizations that once had the talent, technology, and ambition to lead their industries atrophy— not dramatically or publicly, but silently, dangerously, from comfort. Comfort, the quiet killer of transformation, comes from executives who haven't **re-earned** their roles in decades, innovation committees producing nothing but paperwork, and processes disguised as rigorous oversight and yet designed to delay uncomfortable decisions.

This comfort breeds stagnation. Internally, creativity stalls under bureaucratic friction, risk is not managed but avoided, and decisions are postponed so long that markets move ahead without us. Externally, executives keep speaking disruptively, yet the company moves sluggishly, a dinosaur pretending to be agile.

Leadership is not about having all the answers or being the smartest in the room; it's about creating conditions in which the smartest people thrive. It's protecting momentum, not egos. When leaders fail, consequences ripple outward, opportunities vanish, teams disengage, and talented individuals depart silently.

This is how transformation dies, with a thousand shrugged shoulders, endless deferrals, and leaders who believe silence is safer than honesty and political positioning is more valuable than meaningful action.

This mirage, seductive yet empty, is most visible in the corporate world. Beneath slick investor briefings, glossy reports, and self-congratulatory LinkedIn posts lies an uncomfortable reality: expensive projects abandoned, flashy technologies quietly retired, and internal systems held together by workarounds and exhausted engineers.

Only by confronting these truths honestly, beyond buzzwords and headlines, can genuine transformation occur.

Until then, we chase illusions, waste talent, and betray those who believe their work could be meaningful. This is a cost we cannot afford.

Chapter 2: Leadership Unfit for the Digital Age

The Rise of the Overprivileged Leader

There's a certain kind of silence that fills a room when someone is promoted and everyone knows they didn't earn it.

It's not the reverent hush reserved for excellence, nor the admiring quiet that follows a remarkable achievement. It's heavier. It's the kind of silence that sinks into your bones, signaling resignation, disbelief, and confirmation of what too many employees suspect but wish wasn't true: EFFORT ALONE WILL NEVER BE ENOUGH.

I've felt that silence more times than I care to remember.

A leader steps forward, someone who's never managed through a crisis, never shipped a meaningful product, never navigated real complexity with grace. And yet, here they are, smiling with the calm assurance of someone who has never had to doubt their ascent. They're chosen not for their courage or clarity, but because they've lingered long enough in the right rooms. They know how to charm at dinners, how to nod at the right moments, and how to be remembered without ever risking too much.

These are not leaders in the traditional sense. They are passengers on a corporate conveyor belt, rising not through accomplishment but through comfort. They're experts in optics and proximity, not innovation or stewardship. They've mastered the art of being visible without being vulnerable, of deflecting accountability while accumulating praise. They're not here to lead transformation; they're here to maintain the conditions that keep them safe.

And yes, though it stings to say out loud, they often carry other unspoken privileges: the "right" accent, the "right" color, the "right" school, the "right" cultural fluency that puts senior leaders at ease. The organization may preach meritocracy and diversity, but behind closed doors, privilege still acts like a passport. Credentials are weighted differently depending on who holds them. A degree from the right institution in Boston or London will be lauded; the same degree from any institution abroad will be scrutinized. A polished accent will be praised for leadership presence; a foreign cadence will be flagged for "communication coaching."

This credentialism is not just inconsistent; it's also deeply political. Insiders, groomed over years of strategic friendships, can coast on loyalty alone. Outsiders, especially immigrants, people of color, or those unwilling to play politics, must carry twice the weight just to stand still. I've seen engineers capable of architecting brilliant systems sidelined, not because of incompetence, but because they were marked as "too technical," "too blunt," or "not leadership material." Not for what they lacked, but for what they threatened.

This is where nepotism evolves into something even more dangerous: *preservationism*. In small companies, nepotism is overt; the founder's "golden child" gets the role. But in large corporations, it can be more subtle. Promotions are justified through relationships, "cultural fit," and "trust." Roles are carved out to insulate power, not to deliver impact. Diversity programs are repurposed to cloak the status quo, shielding decision-makers from real accountability.

Leadership becomes a reward for allegiance, not a responsibility to steward. And slowly, the organization begins to rot.

Real transformation requires discomfort. It demands that leaders be willing to hear hard truths, to be challenged by people smarter or bolder than themselves. But when leadership is chosen for comfort, transformation becomes impossible. Organizations then fall into a kind of stasis: vibrant on the outside, hollow at the core. They alienate exceptional talent, replace real diversity with tokenism, and swap bold possibilities for safe compromises.

Then, inevitably, when urgency strikes, when markets shift or crises emerge, these leaders are unprepared. No one has ever told them the truth. No one has ever pushed back. They are surrounded by people trained to agree, not to think. And when the moment comes that demands vision, all they can offer are slogans.

This dynamic isn't new. Laurence J. Peter named it in 1969 as the "Peter Principle," stating that people rise to their level of incompetence.[1] But in the context of digital transformation, this phenomenon becomes catastrophic. Promotions are based on past familiarity, not future readiness. And the higher these leaders climb, the more brittle their reality becomes.

They cling to outdated achievements like heirlooms, recycling the same war story from 2015, the same metrics from a sunset project, as if relevance has no expiration date. They stop learning. They stop listening. Growth becomes optional and then invisible.

Comfort, once a reward, becomes a prison. Accountability fades. Feedback disappears. Privileges remain until the day the system breaks, and the leaders meant to guide us through the storm don't even realize it's raining.

Technology vs. Power Politics

When digital transformation efforts stall, the scapegoat is almost always technology, the vendor, the platform, the data quality. These are easy targets, abstract enough to blame and complex enough to avoid scrutiny.

But more often than not, the real problem isn't technical. It's political.

I've seen brilliant technical solutions tossed aside because they threatened someone's narrative. Proposals that could have saved millions were quietly buried because they came from the wrong person or circumvented the favored committee. Meanwhile, weaker, politically safe initiatives moved forward, wasting time and resources while protecting egos.

Technology should be neutral, an amplifier of clarity, a tool for value creation. But in many organizations, it becomes weaponized. Innovation becomes a threat. Engineers enter rooms with clean logic and thoughtful trade-offs, but by the time those ideas pass through the executive filter, they emerge twisted, sanitized, delayed, or erased entirely.

Roadmaps are rewritten without explanation. Priorities shift for no discernible reason. Decisions happen behind closed doors, not for strategic alignment but for personal protection. The message to innovators becomes chillingly clear: Excellence is expendable if it makes the wrong person uncomfortable.

This is not transformation. It's political theater with a better UX.

When politics wins, innovation loses. Because politics prizes safety. Technology demands truth. The two are incompatible when truth threatens power.

The cost isn't just in failed projects or missed deadlines. It's in morale. Talent. Trust. People stop trying. The boldest thinkers leave. The brightest ideas never see daylight. A culture of learned helplessness sets in, where ambition is punished and caution is rewarded.

This isn't a broken system; it's a hostage situation. Talent, innovation, and opportunity are all held captive by a leadership culture afraid to be uncomfortable.

A Glimpse Beyond the Mirage

But there is another way.

Real leadership in the digital age doesn't mean having the best idea in the room. It means creating a room where the best ideas can emerge and survive. It means building systems where truth flows upward, not just status. Where dissent is a form of care. Where credentials are earned through impact, not aesthetics.

The leaders who thrive in transformation aren't always the most polished. But they are the most honest. They listen. They adapt. They know when to step back and let others lead. They welcome complexity because they know that simplicity born from fear is far more dangerous than the messiness of change.

These leaders are rare. But they exist.

They are the ones who will carry us forward, if we let them lead.

As we move into Chapter 3, we'll explore what happens when these two instincts collide: the instinct to protect comfort, and the instinct to confront change. And why, if we don't learn to embrace discomfort as the raw material of transformation, we risk losing not just our edge, but also our integrity.

Chapter 3: The Theater of Avoidance

Political Solutions to Technological Problems

It's always startling how quickly a boardroom can transform into a theater of politics the moment a genuinely complex technical issue enters the conversation. Not the polished, consultant-friendly complexity that fits neatly into a strategy deck, but the messy kind. The kind layered with systems history, architectural interdependencies, and acronyms that whisper how long we've been avoiding the truth.

In one institution I worked with, I watched a leadership team spend three months debating the difference between a "mobile wallet" and a "digital wallet." Not because the nuance was paralyzing, but because no leader in the room had the technical fluency to make a confident call. So, they did what they'd been conditioned to do: defer to process, retreat to posturing, and mask confusion with PowerPoint.

Another quarter was lost in circular deliberation over whether to adopt a Token Service Provider (TSP), a foundational security layer for digital payments. The stall wasn't about risk. It was about fear. Fear of being wrong. Fear of being seen. Fear of surrendering control in a domain where politics could no longer pretend to lead.

After one particularly hollow meeting, an architect confided in me:

"We weren't designing infrastructure anymore. We were designing presentations."

This wasn't a breakdown of decision-making; it was a collapse of courage.

Where Complexity Meets Ego

The true obstacle isn't technology. It's what complexity reveals: fragile egos, leadership insecurity, and the deep human resistance to being a beginner again. Many executives who once rose through sharp operational instincts now find themselves unmoored in a digital world they don't understand, and rather than learn, they leverage. Committees bloom like weeds. Consultants are brought in not to illuminate, but to insulate. Critical choices are delayed until they become politically convenient instead of strategically urgent.

Momentum suffers first. But what withers more quietly is trust.

Engineers disengage. Architects stop arguing. Product leads begin padding timelines, not out of apathy, but for survival. The emotional tone shifts, curiosity dulls, optimism shrinks, and that slow, quiet heartbreak begins.

A developer on a Brazilian core banking project told me: "We warned them the timeline was too aggressive. But nobody wanted to move the investor date. After a while, I stopped talking. What was the point?"

That's not attrition of skill. It's attrition of spirit. And once belief is gone, belief that your leadership sees you, hears you, you can't win it back with a town hall or a values slide.

There is no shortcut around complexity. The only way is through. And that demands a rare kind of leadership: one willing to sit in discomfort, admit what it doesn't know, and build genuine fluency across layers of the organization.

This chapter isn't an indictment of ignorance. It's a call to humility. Because the most dangerous leaders in the digital age aren't the ones who don't understand technology. They're the ones who pretend they do.

The Cost of Misaligned Agendas

Worse than incompetence is misalignment, the distortion of organizational energy around appearances rather than outcomes.

Too often, technology becomes a prop in a political play. Leadership greenlights shiny initiatives to signal progress: a chatbot here, a slick interface there. But under the surface, systems are taped together, fragile and incoherent. These aren't strategies. They're stagecraft.

And what's lost isn't just budget; it's also infrastructure. It's cohesion. It's the hard, often invisible work that makes innovation sustainable.

Once the confetti settles, it's delivery teams who are left to stitch together the consequences, in silence, while credit flows upward and sideways.

As a lead engineer from a failed digital wallet rollout in India put it:

"We had three systems doing the same job. And four leaders claimed victory. Meanwhile, we were firefighting every day."

This isn't dysfunction. It's design. Misalignment rewards speed over sense. Visibility over value. Political dexterity over engineering integrity.

Technologists are demoted from partners to plumbers, brought in late, blamed when things break, excluded from timelines they'll later be held accountable to. Strategy becomes performative. Burnout becomes structural. And transformation becomes a punchline whispered between engineers who've seen this movie before.

Global Failures, Local Variations

This is not a regional issue. It's a global pattern with localized expressions.

In the United States, Evolve Bank & Trust's systems collapsed under the strain of unchecked fintech scaling. The breach wasn't just technical; it was also cultural. Senior leaders resigned not over failure, but over the lack of courage and integrity in the aftermath.[2]

In the United Kingdom, TSB's 2018 IT meltdown locked out millions. Repeated warnings were ignored in the rush to meet a self-imposed deadline. As one insider put it, "It was a failure of honesty, not engineering."[3]

In India, Punjab National Bank lost $2 billion, not just to fraudsters, but also to institutional inertia. Aging systems, left untouched to avoid internal conflict, eventually snapped.[4]

In Brazil, a digital bank's core upgrade went live to meet investor optics, not engineering readiness. The result: months of outages. Engineers had warned leadership. "We knew it would break," one said. "Just not how badly."[5]

The languages and rituals differ—polish in New York, politeness in London, deference in Delhi, charisma in São Paulo—but the outcome is the same: technology warped by ego, speed, and spin.

The Hidden Cost: Fear, Fatigue, and Disbelief

At its core, this isn't about technology. It's about fear.

Not fear of failure, but fear of inadequacy. Of being revealed. Of losing control in rooms where certainty is currency.

This fear calcifies into politics. But the cost is cumulative.

Projects stall. Promises erode. Talent disengages—not because people lack resilience, but because they no longer believe their effort will be honored. They stop dreaming. Then they stop trying.

The most dangerous trait in any organization is not

ignorance; it's evasion. The inability to face discomfort, contradiction, and complexity with honesty.

And beneath that lies the real crisis: a persistent skills gap in corporate leadership. Leaders don't understand how technology works, and they also don't know how to lead when they don't understand.

That's the new leadership test:
- Can you hold uncertainty without weaponizing it?
- Can you absorb discomfort without numbing it with jargon?
- Can you walk into a room where you are no longer the expert, and still lead?

In Chapter 4, we'll examine the leadership pipeline itself and learn why the traits that once defined high potential are now liabilities in a digital world. We'll explore how operational excellence and political fluency have been mistaken for transformation readiness, and what it means to lead from complexity rather than legacy.

Because the future doesn't need perfect leaders. It needs honest ones.

Chapter 4: The Skills Gap in Corporate Leadership

Ignoring the New Basics

There's a kind of confidence that comes only from not knowing what's at stake.

We were deep into a critical review of our digital payment's roadmap, a complex but essential upgrade that would allow for real-time settlement, new wallet integrations, and more resilient compliance tracing. The technical path had been scoped. Dependencies mapped. Risks documented. The team presenting, diverse, experienced, and exceptionally sharp, had prepared for weeks. Engineers, product leaders, and compliance architects had collaborated across time zones to frame the opportunity clearly: a new payment feature that would open new revenue streams while finally modernizing our archaic settlement flow.

We had one hour on the calendar with the executive sponsor, a senior leader with undeniable presence and a career built on operational achievements. But also, someone who hadn't coded, architected, or managed a technical product in years. Still, he walked in with the confidence of someone ready to decide. Or so we thought.

Ten minutes into the meeting, it became clear he hadn't read the deck. Fifteen minutes in, after a brief but clear technical explanation, he paused. Nodded. And then he did what so many leaders in traditional corporations do when faced with something outside their comfort zone: *He invited more people.*

"We need to bring in Jeff [from marketing]," he said. "And I think Charles [from risk] and Amanda [from legal] need to weigh in on this feature before we make any calls."

It was a payment authorization toggle. Already cleared by risk. Already vetted by legal. We weren't launching a new product; we were flipping a switch. Still, he insisted.

At that moment, the game was no longer about clarity or consensus. It was about deference, about reinforcing who mattered in the room. He didn't say "marketing needs to weigh in" or "we should align with legal." He named people. Because in these environments, hierarchy is not a function; it's a performance. It's a subtle reminder of who carries weight and who doesn't. For those who thrive in that order, names are power. Titles are currency. And ambiguity is armor.

This ritual, summoning more names, more voices, more visibility, masquerades as thoroughness. But it's often a stall. A delay tactic. A power move to ensure that no decision happens outside the gravitational pull of senior comfort.

And for the teams doing the actual work, it lands like a gut punch.

One product manager told me:

"I stopped prepping for decision meetings. They weren't really for decisions. They were for proving who hadn't been looped in yet."

Instead of solving a problem, we were solving for attendance. We were trying to align thirty-five calendars across five time zones, all in service of re-discussing a toggle that had already been reviewed, documented, and approved. The meeting ended not with clarity, but with twelve new action items, most of which involved rewording things we'd already agreed on. We weren't progressing; we were pretending.

In these moments, two types of people reveal themselves. The first are those who've adapted to inefficiency, not because they believe in it, but because they've learned how to game it. They nod at the busywork. They pretend these tasks matter. Deep down, they know it's just a month of drift disguised as diligence, time to coast beneath the banner of "alignment."

And then there are the others. The ones who still believe in the work. For them, these meetings don't just waste time.

They wound. Because to care is to suffer. And to speak up is to risk being labeled difficult, impatient, or "not a team player."

One engineer later whispered to me, "You either join the theater, or you get written out of the script."

And yet, even here, there are those who refuse to give up. Quiet rebels who push forward in small, strategic ways. Who mentor quietly. Who shield their teams from chaos. They keep the soul of the organization alive, even when its structure forgets them.

Four weeks later, the same issue was resolved in seven minutes. Not because anything had changed, but because the right names were finally in the room. Presence, not logic, moved the needle. The message was clear: Decisions don't hinge on clarity; they hinge on proximity to power.

The Hidden Cost of Digital Illiteracy

This is what happens when leadership lacks digital fluency. Not just technical knowledge, but the ability to distinguish between complexity and excuses. Between risk and fear. Between necessary alignment and manufactured delay. They don't merely slow projects down. They drain rooms of urgency. And eventually, they drain people of purpose.

Digital fluency isn't about knowing how to code. It's about knowing when to defer to those who do. It's about understanding how systems integrate, how dependencies form, how technical risk compounds if ignored. It's the ability to listen without deflecting, to decide without dramatizing, and to lead without centering oneself in every decision.

Overvaluing Soft Power

If digital illiteracy is the engine of stagnation, then soft power is its mask. The ability to speak fluently in "executive tone" has become a substitute for actual insight. The result? People who solve problems become invisible, while those who narrate them with flair become indispensable.

This is not to say that soft power has no place. Influence, communication, and trust-building are essential. But when those qualities outweigh technical understanding, when charisma replaces competence, organizations become fragile. Visibility becomes currency, and those closest to the real problems are kept farthest from the solution.

Performing Progress: The Rise of Bullshit Jobs

In legacy institutions, theatre often replaces transformation. Dashboards, slide decks, workshops, and color-coded charts become ends in themselves. This is choreography, not change. These are the "bullshit jobs" David Graeber warned about,[6] roles created not out of necessity but to sustain the illusion of momentum.

I once attended a "program celebration" with twelve "deliverables" that included a rebranded internal tool no one used and a training session no one attended. Everyone clapped. The leader beamed. But the core system? Still broken. Still untouched.

Yet I've seen real transformation, too. I've seen engineers who rewrite infrastructure with elegance and scale. Product leads who say no to political pressure. Designers who insist on usability over optics. When they're empowered, magic happens. Velocity returns. Trust deepens. Teams surge.

The Slow Collapse of Meaning

When facade becomes default, people stop resisting. They protect themselves instead. The lead architect stops pushing. The product owner retreats into silence. Initiative becomes a liability. And when the project finally fails, blame falls downward, not on the indecision above, but on the disengagement below.

This is how meaning erodes. Not through rebellion, but through recalibration. And when caring becomes a cost, only the reckless or the resigned continue to offer it freely.

But it doesn't have to be this way. Organizations can rediscover their spark. Leaders can learn. I've seen them do it. I've worked with execs who admitted their blind spots, invited real dialogue, and let go of the need to appear infallible. When that happens, rooms change. Teams rise.

The future belongs to those who can navigate complexity with humility, not posture. In Chapter 5, we'll explore what I call The Empire Cycle. It's a framework inspired by fourteenth-century historian Ibn Khaldun, who explained that empires don't collapse from external threats, but from within. We'll examine the rituals, myths, and habits that protect legacy thinking, even as the world demands reinvention. Because transformation doesn't begin with tools or frameworks. It begins with truth, and the courage to question the empire we've built around comfort.

Chapter 5: The Empire Cycle

The Cultural Disconnect

There's a point in the life of every organization when the biggest threat isn't competition. It's the culture.

It doesn't happen overnight. At first, culture is a source of strength. It binds people together, helps them move fast, make decisions, and trust each other. But over time, something shifts. The culture that once sparked innovation starts demanding obedience. The rituals that once meant belonging turn into boxes to check. And without realizing it, the organization stops evolving. It starts protecting itself instead.

This slow decay has been happening for centuries.

In the fourteenth century, long before the modern corporation existed, a North African historian named Ibn Khaldun observed something timeless. He studied the rise and fall of dynasties and empires through wars, politics, and patterns of human behavior. What he found was startling: Empires don't collapse because they're conquered. They collapse because they decay from within.

His theory, now known as the Asabiyyah cycle [7], begins with cohesion and necessity. Early rulers are close to the struggle. They fight, build, and lead from urgency. Their unity is forged in hardship. But as the empire grows comfortable, that cohesion dissolves. Later generations inherit wealth, not wisdom. Power, not purpose. And with each passing era, leadership grows more detached, more performative, more ornamental.

Eventually, the rituals of power remain, but the spirit is gone.

That cycle, the predictable arc of rise, comfort, and decay, is what I call The Empire Cycle. It is the quiet undoing of once-great cultures by the very systems they built to preserve themselves. The modern corporation doesn't fall to armies. It falls to inertia. It dies not with a crash, but with a sigh.

Culture as an Inheritance

Most companies don't stop to ask: What kind of culture did we inherit? They assume culture is fixed, part of the brand, part of the story. But culture is more like soil. It holds a memory. It shapes everything that grows from it.

And if that soil hasn't been turned over in a while, if it's full of old habits, rigid hierarchies, and silent rules, then even the boldest ideas will struggle to take root.

Take Maya. She was the first product manager at a fintech startup: scrappy, resourceful, sleeping under her desk during launches, solving real problems in real time. She knew every client's name. Fast forward six years, and she's now a VP in a large, complex corporate structure. Her days are filled with alignment meetings and performance dashboards. When she proposes a bold, user-driven pilot at an executive summit, it's met with silence. Bureaucracy swallows the idea. The betrayal she feels isn't just organizational; it's personal. The same culture that once rewarded creativity now punishes disruption.

She begins to doubt herself. Maybe she was naive. Maybe change is just a younger person's game. Her spark dims, not because she burned out, but because the culture made sure she couldn't burn bright.

Traditional vs. Agile: A Clash of Worlds

Old corporate cultures value control. Plans are made at the top, passed down in presentations, measured in KPIs. There's comfort in predictability, even if it means things move slowly.

Agile cultures, on the other hand, thrive on adaptability. They run on trust, collaboration, and learning in real time. Mistakes aren't punished; they're expected. The goal isn't to control outcomes, but to stay close to reality and respond quickly.

Put those two together in the same organization, and you get friction. Raj, for instance, leads an agile team inside a century-old insurer. They're building digital claims tools at speed. But every step requires approvals, simulations, and oversight. His squad pushes updates on Monday. By Tuesday, they're told to slow down. "We need consensus." Progress loses to process. Momentum fades. The agile team becomes a theater of speed surrounded by a fortress of caution.

Raj begins to feel like an actor in a play no one believes in. His team builds prototypes that never see the light of day. He used to feel like a change agent. Now he just feels tired.

This isn't just a process problem. It's a culture problem. And culture always wins.

The Empire Cycle in Leadership

The Empire Cycle doesn't just shape organizations. It shapes the people who lead them.

In the early days, leaders are scrappy. They build things from scratch, make mistakes, take risks. They know what it's like to be on the ground, close to the customer, close to the consequences.

But as the company grows, leadership becomes more polished. More political. Leaders start inheriting roles rather than earning them in the fire. They rise by mastering the system, not by questioning it.

And in our age, that ascent isn't just internal, it's theatrical. Once someone reaches a certain level, the real work often takes a back seat to the performance of leadership.

Sam did just that. Once an engineer who coded deep into the night, he rose to CTO. In the beginning, he still rolled up his sleeves. Still asked dumb questions. But over time, his focus shifted. He was invited to speak at events; his face was printed in glossy company decks. His social media following grew. He became a brand, an "authority" on technology.

At first, it felt like recognition. Then it became expectation. And finally, it became the job. He started managing optics more than outcomes. He crafted narratives that were neat, digestible, and applauded. When challenged in a strategy meeting, he didn't ask what he was missing. He defended what he had said.

Slowly, without realizing it, he had gone from builder to steward. From steward to symbol. From influencer to insulation.

And he was not alone.

In today's digital corporate landscape, ego has become a currency. Leaders feed it. Companies exploit it. The "40 under 40 in tech." The "Latinos in Fintech." The "Men or Women in Payments" awards. Bright stages, spotlight panels, LinkedIn algorithms designed to reward self-celebration. It's not that recognition is inherently bad. But when it becomes the goal, the work suffers.

Consulting and Marketing companies know this. Some even engineer it. Ego is a sales funnel now. Companies build platforms that amplify executives, hoping the spotlight will convert into contracts. They curate shows, sponsor interviews, post glamorized portraits of leaders who say all the right things, but rarely challenge the system that protects them.

And orbiting this ecosystem are the consultants, the so-called "objective voices" who often become co-authors of the illusion.

These firms don't just advise. They validate. They produce glossy reports that echo what leadership already believes, not what the market actually demands. Their analysis is often less about truth than alignment. It's designed not to provoke transformation, but to protect reputations.

Cherry-picked data. Skewed forecasts. Strategic silence around inconvenient insights.

And more often than not, these relationships aren't forged in intellectual rigor. They're built on proximity. Familiarity. Old friendships from business school. A former colleague is now at the firm. A board member made the intro. It's not formal nepotism, but the dynamic is the same.

This is how the overprivileged and underqualified keep finding their way to the table: They didn't earn their seat, but they already knew someone sitting there. Expertise becomes secondary. What matters is access. Polish. The ability to speak the language of power without ever questioning its terms.

So, what should be a crucible of critical thinking becomes a mirror hall of mutual reinforcement. Leaders perform insight. Consultants perform rigor. Everyone gets what they came for, except the truth.

And the Empire Cycle spins on.

Resistance to Change: The Quiet Defense of the Status Quo

Here's the hard truth: Most resistance to change isn't loud. It's subtle.

It's in a meeting where no one challenges the plan. It's in the executive who nods but never follows through. It's in the well-meaning manager who delays a new idea because "the timing isn't right" or "we don't want to rock the boat."

Nina felt it firsthand. A passionate division head, she launched a client-centric pilot rooted in bold, personal design. Her team was energized. The data looked promising. But at every executive touchpoint, the message was the same: "Let's revisit." "Refine the ROI." "Interesting, but..."

Each delay was couched in professionalism. Each meeting diluted the momentum. And eventually, Nina's team gave up. The fire went out.

Resistance doesn't look like rebellion. It looks like a polite delay.

And it often comes from the top, not because leaders are malicious, but because change is uncomfortable. It threatens the systems they know. The power they hold. The stories they tell about themselves.

Real transformation asks leaders to give up control. To admit they don't have all the answers. To be changed by the process. That's not a strategy shift. That's an identity shift.

And without it, the Empire Cycle rolls on.

The Quiet Descent

None of this feels dramatic. That's the danger.

There are no headlines. No clear villain. Just smart people inside smart companies quietly reinforcing the past, even as they speak about the future. It looks like continuity. But indeed, it's decline.

And decline doesn't always look like failure. It often arrives dressed as maturity. It calls itself synergy. Integration. Global reach. But behind the buzzwords is a story that plays out again and again: two legacy cultures, each clinging to their past, collide and collapse inward.

Take Nokia and Siemens. When their network divisions merged in the mid-2000s, it was painted as a power move.[8] Nokia, still a global leader, was riding high on mobile dominance. Siemens, older and more burdened by layers of hierarchy, had already started to lose its edge. Beneath the surface, both companies were deep into the Empire Cycle, but moving at different speeds.

Siemens had stopped listening years before. Leadership had become risk-averse, process-bound, loyal to form over function. The company had brilliant engineers, but their voices were drowned out by politics.

Nokia, meanwhile, still had market momentum, but its

internal culture was already shifting. Decisions slowed. Risk tolerance dropped. Vision got buried under success.

The merger created Nokia Siemens Networks. But instead of revitalization, it accelerated decline. The combined entity inherited the worst of both worlds: bloated governance, conflicting identities, and a cautious, self-protective culture. Innovation slowed. Focus blurred. People left.

One insider described the post-merger culture as "a meeting of two ghosts." The rooms were full, but the spirit was gone.

Eventually, Nokia began to recover. Stripped of its consumer phone business, it reinvented itself with a renewed focus on next-generation network infrastructure. The company transformed. It found purpose. But that came with steep costs: the loss of legacy markets, an internal reinvention, and a painful reckoning with its past.

Thousands of jobs were lost. Not because the technology failed. Not because the market dried up. But because leadership failed to lead.

This is the cost of the Empire Cycle: not just missed opportunities, but broken careers. Disbanded teams. Cultures erased. The empire still stands, but the spirit is gone. And so we arrive at the edge of the cliff, not with a scream, but with a shuffle.

Most companies don't collapse in flames. They shrink. They merge. They quietly sell off the parts that once made them great. And if they survive, they do so as smaller, safer, more forgettable versions of themselves. The culture that once set them apart is hollowed out, replaced with polite compliance, diluted passion, and the relentless hum of business as usual.

The tragedy of the Empire Cycle is not just its predictability; it's also how rarely it is interrupted.

Yet decline isn't destiny. Empires that recognize their own decay have a choice: to double down on appearances, or to rediscover purpose. But that takes humility. And humility, in most boardrooms, remains the rarest form of courage.

We've seen how this plays out inside companies. But it isn't just about isolated firms. Entire sectors are infected. And few more so than financial services.

The symptoms are masked by capital, by regulation, by tradition. But make no mistake: The industry is in crisis, not of solvency, but of spirit.

Chapter 6 begins here, with a look at the corporate world crisis as a cultural reckoning. Because if we want to understand why transformation keeps failing, we must look beyond the org charts and into the soul of the system.

Chapter 6: The Legacy Traditional Sector in Crisis

Not a technical problem, but a cultural reckoning.

Transformation in traditional industries doesn't falter because of bad tech. It falters because of deeply held beliefs. Because somewhere inside the architecture of these long-standing institutions, beneath the polished strategy decks and compliance frameworks, there's quiet but powerful inertia. A cultural immune system, built up over decades, defending tradition against disruption.

This chapter isn't about failed digitization projects or missed deadlines. It's about something more intimate and harder to measure: the collective psychology of organizations straddling two worlds. On one side, there's the weight of legacy, outdated systems, conservative governance, and layers of protocol. On the other, there's the accelerating demands of digital-native competition, shifting customer expectations, and regulatory environments that now require both transparency and agility.

To understand why transformation keeps stalling in these corporations, we must look beyond processes and into the cultural DNA of the system.

The Logic of Legacy

Legacy isn't just a system or a structure. It's a mindset, a way of relating to risk, to time, to power. It sees the future through the lens of precedent. It trusts what is known (even if it's outdated) over what is possible (even if it's necessary). *Legacy mindset believes safety lies in predictability, not in adaptation.* It rewards those who remember the rules, not those who question them.

This mindset didn't arise by accident. It was built for a different era, when consistency was king and risk was linear. But in a nonlinear world, the logic of legacy becomes a liability. It resists feedback. It pathologizes failure. And when disruption comes, whether from startups, regulation, or customer expectation, it flinches instead of flexing.

A Sector Behind the Curve

These organizations aren't lagging because they lack ambition. They're lagging because they were built to resist change. Years, sometimes centuries, of risk-averse decision-making have fostered cultures that reward caution and penalize deviation. Compliance is a virtue; curiosity is a liability.

Take, for instance, the case of a century-old insurance company headquartered in the Midwest. When their innovation team proposed piloting an AI-driven underwriting process, they met with what seemed like open-minded approval. A budget was allocated. A vendor was brought in. But six months later, the pilot was dead, not because the technology failed, but because every internal compliance review added a new layer of complexity. The legal team feared precedent, the operations group feared instability, and senior leaders feared reputational risk. Eventually, what started as an experiment became a cautionary tale. The innovation lead, exhausted and disillusioned, left within the year.

Yes, regulatory burdens are real. And yes, legacy systems can be technological minefields. But the deeper issue isn't infrastructure. It's mindset. Many of these institutions still define competence through control rather than creativity, safety rather than adaptability.

What's often framed as "transformation fatigue" is, at its core, a cultural crisis: teams operating in environments where they're told to innovate but expected to conform.

The Price of Failure

And the cost of that contradiction? It's visible everywhere. Outdated customer experiences that drive disengagement. Internal talent that quietly exits after one too many false starts. A creeping cynicism that undermines even the most earnest efforts at change.

I saw this firsthand in a pilot project involving voice recognition technology to approve payments while driving your car. It was a bold idea, cutting-edge, intuitive, and potentially transformative. But from the beginning, it was clear we weren't just building a product; we were navigating a labyrinth.

No one had asked for a Scope of Work, yet everyone had opinions. Compliance had a list of concerns. Legal wanted feasibility assessments. Leaders submitted individual requests, often without aligning with each other or even understanding what they were asking for. So, we did what agile teams do best: We proposed a living Scope of Work, one that outlined OKRs, metrics, regulatory checkpoints, and sprint milestones. A blueprint for adaptability.

But instead of unleashing momentum, the document became another arena for political performance. Leaders debated revisions like lawyers parsing a contract. Every change was a defense of territory, not a contribution to progress. Eventually, the scope was finalized, but no one would sign it. Not officially. Not with accountability.

And so, the clock ran out.

Our external partners, patient through six months of inertia, walked away. They took their technology to a firm willing to move at the pace of innovation, not the pace of avoidance. That voice recognition capability exists today. But not in our company. For us, it's a ghost. A reminder that failure doesn't always look like collapse. Sometimes, it looks like hesitation.

A Flicker of Resistance

But even in these systems, not everyone complies.

When we were designing that project, there was one manager—let's call her Ana—who refused to let the idea die. She challenged every delay. She called out the posturing. She brought actual users into the room. For months, she absorbed the frustration of others and turned it into fuel. Her insistence on clarity didn't make her popular, but it made her respected. She didn't win. But she didn't shrink.

And her presence mattered more than the outcome. Cultural change doesn't always start with victory; sometimes, it starts with refusal. Ana reminded us that the fire hadn't gone out. It was just waiting for someone to protect it.

The Human Cost

The danger isn't just that legacy companies fall behind. It's that the people inside them begin to disappear, slowly and imperceptibly. Not through layoffs or resignations, but through quiet disillusionment. Passion gives way to protocol. Initiative shrinks. Creativity flattens.

What these companies fail to understand is that their most powerful asset is not their systems or their compliance frameworks. It's their people. People who, under the right leadership and in the right culture, could thrive. People who know how to collaborate across silos, who care deeply about users and customers, who want to make something better than what came before.

But instead of having the chance to succeed, those people spend their days navigating a labyrinth. Rewriting scopes. Sitting in meetings about metrics no one uses. Hearing "agile" as a slogan, not a practice.

And little by little, the system wears them down.

We start with energy. With belief. We try to change things. But eventually, we learn to play the game. We stay quiet when we should speak. We comply when we should challenge. We compromise when we should walk.

Because we have mortgages to pay. Children to raise. A fragile equilibrium to maintain.

And then comes the cruelest irony: We teach our children to dream, to follow their passions, to find meaning in their work. And they nod, loving us, admiring us, while sensing the tension between what we say and what we've settled for.

We laugh; if we don't, we might break. But inside, we know. We are not just employees. We are captives of responsibility, of expectation, of a system that thrives on our silence.

Maybe it's too late for us. But not for them.

Our hope is that our children might inherit something better. That they might enter organizations where excellence is welcomed, where courage is cultivated, and where transformation is embraced rather than feared.

Until that day comes, we will keep losing not just capability, but also something far more precious.

We'll lose the person who once believed they could change things. We'll lose the young dreamer who wanted to make systems more just. The teammate who believed in shared purpose. The builder who stayed late, not for applause, but for pride.

Instead of allowing them to fulfill their potential, we ask them to comply. To perform. To adapt to a culture that punishes integrity and rewards loyalty to comfort. And slowly, they give in and stay. But not as they were.

This isn't just stagnation. It's a betrayal of what work could be, of what it *should* be. But belief isn't gone. It's waiting. Waiting for someone to protect it. To fan it back to life. The cycles can be broken. But only if we start with the one force that shapes everything, from tone to trust, from vision to value: leadership.

Chapter 7: Breaking the Cycle: A Blueprint for Change

The quiet revolution has already begun.

It didn't start in boardrooms. It didn't come from panels or keynote speeches or award ceremonies. It wasn't the result of quarterly innovation challenges or leadership off-sites. It began in overlooked corners. In quiet rebellions. In fleeting acts of care, in someone explaining patiently, offering encouragement, or simply noticing what others missed. It began in Slack messages. In late-night sprints. In whispered solidarity between people who refused to let cynicism win.

It started with builders. People who still believe that work could be sacred. That leadership could be earned, not inherited. Those systems, however broken, however calcified, could still be rewritten, not by permission, but by participation.

These people believe in legacy, but not the kind built on titles and tenure. They believe in the kind built on impact, on people, on the work itself. This revolution is not loud, but it is relentless. And it is already here.

This chapter is for the people who are working to break the cycle. And for everyone still carrying hope inside a system that keeps trying to extinguish it.

What Leadership Should Look Like

True digital-era leaders aren't the ones with the loudest voices. They're the ones who listen. Who admit what they don't know. Who elevate the invisible work, not just the visible wins. They're not the ones constantly curating their personal brand online, attending panels, or trading compliments in echo chambers of ego.

Real leaders don't need the spotlight because they are already lit from within by clarity, by vision, and by care. They're not concerned about how they'll be perceived at the next leadership summit. They're concerned about whether their people are aligned, empowered, and seen.

Because they understand something most leaders forget: *The root of most dysfunction isn't incompetence or attitude. It's confusion.*

Lack of clarity is the silent killer of progress. And real leaders know that clarity of purpose, of priorities, of expectations, is their responsibility. They don't outsource it. They don't delegate it. They embody it.

They see the talent others overlook, not because they're scanning résumés, but because they're paying attention to the small acts of brilliance that happen offstage. The intern who quietly untangles a bug that stumped a senior engineer. The analyst who reworks a dashboard over the weekend, not for praise, but because they care. These leaders notice.

They detect the pain points that polite meetings hide. The glance between teammates when a decision makes no sense. The silence that falls too fast after a question no one dares answer. The recurring delay everyone blames on "dependencies" that actually comes from fear.

They see through choreography. They listen between the lines.

And they never assume people are the problem; they understand that systems, when unclear or misaligned, make good people doubt themselves.

Because these leaders have felt it, too: That creeping self-doubt when the metrics don't match the lived reality. That slow erosion of confidence when good work is overlooked and loud work is rewarded. That ache when a brilliant teammate shuts down, not because they've lost their edge, but because they've lost their audience.

These leaders don't punish performance dips. They investigate them. They ask: What's in your way? What do you need from me that you're not getting? Is the structure failing you?

They know that disengagement is often a symptom, not a flaw. That silence is sometimes a survival tactic. And that the best way to "fix" performance is not through pressure, but through clarity, courage, and trust.

In the end, they understand something essential: People want to do meaningful work. People want to matter. And when they don't, it's rarely because they've stopped trying. It's because somewhere along the line, they stopped being seen, being listened to, and vision was replaced by a game of politics.

So, these leaders don't manage by control. They manage by alignment. They remove friction. They tell the truth. And they create systems that whisper to people: You belong here. You're safe here. Let's build something worthy of your talent.

They know that when a team stalls, it's not time for another workshop. It's time for sharper direction; it's time for clearer signals. Not louder voices.

Clarity isn't just a leadership skill. It's the soil from which everything else grows.

Some of these leaders carry titles. Many do not. But you know them when they enter the room, not by the silence they command, but by the space they hold.

They're the ones people turn to when the system breaks, when politics are too loud and the purpose too faint. They are the mentors who share knowledge freely, not to prove what they know, but to lift others higher. They don't protect information like currency. They give it away like light.

I think of Alicia, a senior engineer with no formal leadership role whose quiet presence transformed our entire floor. She never needed to raise her voice. She never sought credit. But she knew how every system worked; she took the time to understand not just the code, but also the people behind it. She wrote documentation late at night so new hires wouldn't struggle. She stayed on calls with junior engineers until they felt safe to take over. Her influence didn't come from authority. It came from trust. And it ran deeper than any org chart could capture.

Or Ian, the product lead who'd seen three CIOs come and go. He didn't speak much in meetings. But when he did, people stopped typing. He was the keeper of institutional memory, not because he hoarded it, but because he gave it away. Freely. Generously. He taught not just tools, but also temperament. He showed what it meant to hold standards without ego, to speak truth without theatrics.

These are the leaders we rarely celebrate. Because their power doesn't come from charisma. It comes from character.

They don't build careers for self-promotion. They build cultures of care. And in a world obsessed with disruption, they remind us of what continuity feels like.

You know them when you meet them. There's a stillness to their presence. A clarity. A warmth. They ask questions that matter. They remember your strengths and skills. They look you in the eye when the project fails and say, "We'll figure it out. Together."

And you find yourself thinking, "I wish you were my boss."

Not because they're perfect. But because they make you better. Because they make the work feel worth it again. Because in their presence, the future doesn't feel so far away.

It starts small. Always. Not with an enterprise-wide reorg or a million-dollar initiative, but with a single choice. A moment where someone chooses to do the braver thing. The uncomfortable thing. The honest thing.

A leader decides to promote a loyalist and, instead of owning that decision transparently by standing behind it or inviting scrutiny, assembles a panel. Not a forum for genuine discussion, but a circle of like-minded peers chosen to echo their bias. And together, they manufacture the appearance of consensus. But beneath the surface, it's still fear in the driver's seat.

Fear of disruption. Fear of discomfort. Fear of that one person who doesn't just nod, but also questions, not because they're difficult, but because they see too clearly. Because they speak truth too plainly. Because their presence demands growth, not performance. Instead of being embraced, they're labeled "not a team player." "Not the right fit."

But what that really means is: They won't play politics. They won't pretend the broken system is fine. They won't trade clarity for comfort.

To people who've built their safety on sameness, that clarity feels dangerous.

But imagine a different choice. One where the leader opens the decision to rigorous, honest debate. Where the panel includes people with differing perspectives, empowered to challenge assumptions, not just validating them. Where promotion is tied to contribution, not allegiance. And where the outcome, whatever it may be, is shaped by clarity, not choreography.

Imagine, instead, if a leader said: "This person challenges me to think differently, and that's exactly what we need."

Imagine if they valued the one who sees the cracks, not just the one who camouflages them. Imagine if they understood that true alignment isn't about uniformity; it's about shared purpose, powered by diverse ways of thinking, building, and being.

Change begins when a leader uses their privilege not to consolidate power, but to distribute it.

As Marcus Aurelius reminds us, the core of leadership lies in acting with clarity and integrity, leading one's life and one's team by virtue, fairness, and thoughtful action.[9] In modern terms, that means creating environments where authority is shared, not hoarded. Where decisions move closer to work. Where clarity, responsibility, and care ripple outward, not downward.

It means tying bonuses not to vanity metrics, but to human outcomes. Team health. Delivery quality. Innovation velocity. Systems impact.

It means performance reviews include not just what leaders deliver, but how they lead. Who they've empowered. What they've changed their mind about. Where they've practiced humility, not just influence.

Imagine a transformation office that doesn't just exist to circulate updates, but to redesign systems. To dismantle bottlenecks. To challenge outdated hierarchies. To put decisions back where they belong: in the hands of people who are close enough to reality to know what's needed.

Recruiting shifts, too. People are chosen not just for polish, but for potential.

You don't need a résumé full of brand names. You need resilience. Hunger. Integrity. You need to have learned through fire. And still be able to listen, to grow, to trust.

Mentorship must evolve, as well. Not mentoring for optics. Not the performative "leadership visibility" programs designed to flatter senior egos. But mentorship that builds futures.

Mentorship that asks:

What kind of world are we preparing them for? Are we teaching them how to survive the system, or how to change it?

Say no to "culture fit." Say yes to "culture evolution."

Hire the person who brings productive tension. Not because they'll be easy, but because they'll make the culture better. The best teams aren't the ones who agree. They're the ones who know how to disagree with trust.

Rewrite the leadership pipeline. Center it around curiosity, humility, and vulnerability. Prioritize those who admit failure. Who unlearn. Who hold complexity without reaching for control.

The future won't be led by those with the slickest slide decks. It will be led by those who ask better questions and stay to listen to the real answers.

Imagine a quarterly executive review where the first question isn't "What did you achieve?"

But instead: "What changed your mind this quarter?"

Imagine an org chart that isn't a pyramid, but a living network. Where influence flows from value, not title. Where leaders move to problems instead of hovering above them. Where anyone, at any level, can shape the future because they're close enough to see it clearly.

And imagine, just imagine, a culture where silence in a

meeting isn't mistaken for agreement but understood as a signal. A flare in the fog. A moment to pause and ask:

"What truth have we made too costly to speak?"

Because clarity isn't loud. But it is powerful. And real change doesn't happen when we move faster. It happens when we move more honestly. When we make space for tension, for translation, for trust.

Imagine feedback systems that evolve, too. Not just with 360-degree, but with neuronal feedback. Continuous. Multi-directional. Interconnected. A living framework where evaluation isn't filtered through hierarchy but illuminated by it.

Too often, dysfunction hides within the folds of power. A VP sets vague goals. A director defends them. A manager absorbs the fallout. The team feels it but says nothing.

The manager gets blamed. Not because they failed, but because they were failed by the system.

That's not accountability. That's scapegoating. The team knows better. They see where the breakdown starts. And they should have a voice. Not just in rating their manager, but also in mapping the whole chain.

Technology already allows this. AI-assisted tools can reveal influence patterns, highlighting who empowers and who obstructs. They can show who creates momentum, and who quietly derails it.

This isn't surveillance. It's insight. It's using the intelligence inside the system to make it healthier, not to protect power. Because we don't need more leadership protection plans. We need more leadership reflection plans.

That's the future. Not just transformation of process, but also of power. Not just better reporting lines, but also braver cultural lines. Lines of sight. Lines of trust. Lines of care. Not just reshaping products, but reshaping how people are seen, heard, and believed.

This is a blueprint, not a checklist. It's a shift from performance to presence. From hierarchy to humanity. From leadership as elevation, to leadership as service.

It won't happen overnight. But it's already unfolding, in quiet corners, courageous choices, and uncelebrated acts of integrity. It lives in the teams who still believe. In the managers who still care. In the systems quietly being reimagined by people who refuse to surrender to mediocrity.

**These next lines? They're for them.
And they're for you.**
They're not waiting for permission.

They're building new rules.

One meeting, one hire, one honest moment at a time.

This isn't naive optimism. This is practiced hope.

The kind forged in late nights.

In quiet exits.

In whispered encouragements passed like lifelines.

The kind of hope that doesn't need applause. Only oxygen.

The kind that remembers: The empire may still stand. But the rebellion is already here.

It speaks softly. It leads quietly. And one day, it will be the story we tell.

Chapter 8: The Role of Accountability

There is a silence more dangerous than dissent: the silence that follows when people stop believing their voices matter.

That's where many organizations are today. Not in crisis or revolution. Not in resignation. They are in preservation.

And it's not about preservation of value or purpose. It's about preservation of power.

They hold on tightly to the last echoes of a system that once worked, back when customer trust was high, competition was low, and market dominance could be maintained by reputation alone. They see the change coming. They feel it in every new fintech platform, every AI-native startup, every line of code they don't understand. But rather than evolve, they dig in.

Not because they're prepared, but because they're afraid to lose control or be exposed. They're afraid that transformation will require them to admit what they don't know.

So, they don't resign. They entrench. They recycle past wins. They perform certainty. They promote comfort. And they reward those who make the old model feel livable, even as it slowly dies.

This preservation isn't passive. It comes dressed as progress. It shows up as a shiny new app or a sleek dashboard, or a digital assistant that says your name and answers your call. But behind the user interface? It's the same brittle, monolithic backend. The same spaghetti-code core. The same inflexible systems that make innovation a chore and agility a myth.

It's digital transformation by cosmetic surgery. The face looks fresh, but the arteries are still clogged. And tragically, the numbers support it. Profitability is strong. Quarterly growth is real. Stockholders are happy. Bonuses are paid. But it's a lie propped up by a broken tradeoff: short-term gain at the long-term expense of customer dignity.

While the business thrives, the customer is trapped in legacy billing cycles, predatory terms, bundled services that serve only the balance sheet, and systems that penalize movement and reward inertia.

That's not strategy; that's a hostage situation.

If customers had a real choice, many would leave. But switching is hard. Rebuilding is exhausting. And for years, the alternatives were just as bad. But here's the beauty, and the irony, of the moment we're in: Emerging technologies are finally putting the customer back at the center. Not because the new generation of entrepreneurs is nobler; many are driven by the same ambition, the same hunger for wealth, the same desire to build their empires. But their path to power is different.

To win, they must empower. To scale, they must simplify. To thrive, they must earn, not assume, customer trust.

Because when your business model depends on the customer's ability to leave, you are forced to build something worth staying for.

Here's the unintentional justice of this moment: Sometimes, greed builds the tools that set us free. The same drive that corrupted the old system is now powering the platforms that will make it obsolete.

And that is why legacy leadership is afraid, not because customers are angry, but because customers are waking up. Once they experience fairness, once they taste control, they won't go back.

Calling Out the Status Quo

Accountability begins with naming what we've allowed to go unnamed. We can start by acknowledging that a full quarter can be lost debating scope language. That a million-dollar "innovation" launch delivers nothing but noise. That transformation offices exist to track metrics, not enable impact. That the people asking hard questions are labeled "difficult," while those avoiding questions are labeled "leadership material."

We've learned to confuse caution with competence and to reward alignment over truth. We praise stability, even as the walls quietly crack. But accountability doesn't live on dashboards. It doesn't live in internal newsletters or staged Q&A sessions. It lives in the moment someone finally says out loud what everyone else is whispering: "This isn't working." "This decision makes no sense." "This delay is about fear, not feasibility."

These moments are rare, and costly, because the system punishes clarity when it isn't convenient. But they're essential, because transformation without accountability is performance art. And performance without truth is how systems rot.

We Need a New Scoreboard

If we want truth to thrive, we need to rethink not just how we lead, but also how we measure leadership itself.

Legacy KPIs reward visibility, not value. They track timelines, not truth. They celebrate "initiatives launched" but ignore "outcomes realized." That's not accountability. That's avoidance dressed up in metrics. So, here's a better scoreboard, a real one:

The Leadership Accountability Scorecard

Metric	What It Really Measures
Time to Decision	How quickly do leaders move, without hiding behind process?
Innovation Adoption Rate	Do new ideas actually stick, or do they just make it to launch day?
High-Performer Selection	Are we uplifting brilliance or rewarding compliance?
High-Performer Retention	Do our best people stay, or do they slowly disappear?
Feedback Quality Index	Are people speaking truth, or just saying what's safe to share?
Cross-Functional Trust Score	Does collaboration feel like alignment or surveillance?
Team Clarity Pulse	Do people know why they're building what they're building?
Escalation Velocity	How fast does confusion turn into clarity, rather than bureaucracy?
Sponsorship Equity	Are promotions going to value creators, or to value protectors?

You cannot fix what you refuse to measure. And
you cannot lead what you refuse to own.

Leadership Is a Mirror, Not a Title

In many corporate settings, leadership is still treated like a crown: a status symbol, polished and worn, conferred by title and tenure. But real leadership is not something bestowed. It's something revealed. And most often, it is revealed under pressure.

True leadership is not about knowing everything. It's not about having the right answer in every meeting or commanding a room with certainty. Instead, it begins with visibility, not just being seen, but also being truly known by the people affected by your decisions. In environments governed by hierarchy, this kind of visibility is rare. Executives often operate behind layers of abstraction: middle management, dashboards, quarterly reviews. The higher a leader rises, the more insulated they become. Feedback arrives filtered, if at all. And when it does, it often reflects what people believe the leader wants to hear, not what they need to know.

In one organization, for instance, internal surveys showed a steady rise in employee engagement scores. But quietly, the attrition rate was climbing. People weren't staying. They were surviving long enough to find an exit. The executives celebrated the data they could see, blind to the story it excluded. This is the danger of metrics without mirrors: They create an illusion of progress while masking the roots of discontent.

Silence, in such contexts, is misread as agreement. Or worse, as loyalty. But often, it signals fear of retribution and fear of futility. Fear that truth-telling will cost more than it's worth. A real leader knows how to read that silence. They don't interpret it as peace. They treat it as a signal to investigate further.

Leadership, at its best, creates rooms where truth can survive, and thrive. These are rooms where disagreement is valued, not merely tolerated. Where people can say, "I don't think this will work," without being labeled difficult. Where a flawed plan isn't pursued for the sake of unity but reconsidered for the sake of integrity.

And when the truth is uncomfortable, as it often is, leaders don't retreat behind spin or silence. They lean in. They acknowledge oversight, they share responsibility, they recommit to work. "I missed this." "Let's fix it together." "Hold me to it." These are not admissions of weakness. They are declarations of strength.

Accountability Belongs to Everyone, But It Must Start at the Top

Too often, companies invest in superficial tools to foster accountability: empowerment workshops, values posters, team-building days. But none of this matters if the leadership doesn't model what they preach. Employees don't need another motivational slogan about ownership. They need to see it practiced at the highest levels.

It shows up in product decisions. A customer doesn't need a loyalty program with more perks if the core service is broken. They need transparency. Contracts they can understand. Channels that work. Options that respect their time. It's the same with employees. They don't need ping-pong tables or pizza on Fridays if their voices are ignored and their growth is stunted.

And what about shareholders? They, too, play a role. The market still rewards leaders for protecting the status quo, even when it's corroding beneath the surface. True accountability challenges this dynamic. It asks whether we are rewarding the right behaviors. Whether quarterly gains are masking long-term losses in trust, ethics, and resilience.

Because accountability is not just about getting things done. It's about doing the right things for the right reasons. It's about the moral credibility of our institutions. About whether those institutions still deserve the trust people place in them.

From Callouts to Call-Ins

The best organizational cultures don't rely on fear of enforcing standards. They don't shame individuals when things go wrong. Instead, they cultivate conditions where mistakes can be seen early, before those mistakes metastasize into crises. The best organizational cultures create space for dissent, not because it makes people comfortable, but because it keeps the system honest.

In these environments, feedback is not a weapon. It's a form of care. Accountability is not a trap. It's a shared commitment. When someone flags an issue, they are not undermining authority; they are reinforcing integrity.

That's not just a nicer way to work. It's also a smarter one. Because the future is built not on flawless execution, but on adaptive learning. Cultures that can correct themselves quickly will outlast those that perform perfection while suppressing truth.

The Audacity of Responsibility

We don't need more buzzwords. We need more bravery. Not just clear goals on paper, but courageous conversations in rooms where it matters. The strongest organizations are not those with the glossiest reports or the most charismatic leaders. They are those where the truth moves freely. Where decisions are made in daylight. Where failure is not hidden but held up as a shared lesson.

This is what real transformation demands. Not just strategy, but also sincerity. Not just innovation, but also introspection.

The performance era is ending. You can't facelift your way into the future. The age of presence is not about being perfect. It's about being real. And the future doesn't belong to those who perform the part. It belongs to those brave enough to write their own story.

The Invitation

To every leader still carrying hope, this chapter is for you.

This is not a teardown. It's a rebuild. You are not alone. You are not naive. You are not foolish for wanting to lead with integrity, or for believing that organizations can be places of meaning, not just margin.

Because belief still lives on. In the team that still dares to dream. In the junior engineer who still asks the brave question. In the mentor who says, "I've got your back." And in you.

Let this be our new foundation. Not just systems of accountability, but also systems of faith. Faith in people. Faith in clarity. Faith that even the most brittle cultures can remember what it means to care.

The empire may still stand. But the future belongs to the builders. And the rebellion has already begun.

Chapter 9: The Choice to Deserve It

There's a moment after every keynote, after the deck is closed, the Zoom call ends, the audience claps, and the stage lights dim. A moment when everyone returns to their inbox, to their OKRs, to their performance reviews, and nothing changes.

That's when the silence hits.

The silence after the applause is where most transformation dies. Not because no one cared, but because no one stayed with the discomfort long enough to act on it.

This book isn't a blueprint. It won't give you answers or give you shortcuts. It's a mirror. And mirrors don't solve problems; they show you what's already there.

My hope is that, in these pages, you didn't just see dysfunction or failure. You saw something more personal. A reflection. A tension. A glimpse of your own choices, your own voice, your own quiet reckoning, just as it came to me while writing these words. Because the truth is, if you're reading this, you're probably part of the system I've described. So am I.

We've all had to compromise at some point. To clap politely when we wanted to scream. To rewrite the same proposal for the sixth time. To play the game, even when it made us sick to our stomach.

We're not here because we lacked vision. We're here because we cared enough to stay. Walking away would've been easier, but we still believed change was possible. Somewhere, deep beneath the bureaucracy, the burnout, the backchannels, we believed in the work.

Or, maybe, we're still here because we've become bound by a system that forces us to play, just because we once bought a ticket to watch. And now we don't know how to leave the theater.

So, what happens now?

This is not the end. It's the beginning of choosing something different. Of refusing to reward performative leadership. Of mentoring with honesty, not just ambition. Of building teams that don't just look diverse but truly feel safe. Of making space for brilliance in every accent, every background, every kind that's been overlooked by the old rules.

We don't need perfect leaders. We need honest ones. We don't need more frameworks. We need the courage to use the ones we already have. We don't need another transformation plan. We need a reckoning, personal, cultural, and institutional.

It starts with an honest leadership question. A quiet one. "How did I get here?"

Maybe you followed the rules. Maybe you played the game. Maybe the system was always tilted in your favor. And maybe the world started calling you a leader, and you started believing it. But now, something's shifting. Doubt creeps in. You wonder if you're really adding value or just taking up space.

This chapter is for you. Not to shame. But to offer something sacred: a pause. A mirror. A chance to stop performing and start becoming.

Because all that doubt? It's not your undoing. It's your invitation to stop curating an image and start building competence. To stop being shielded and start being stretched.

When you stay in impostor mode too long, the room adapts around your fear. People stop telling you the truth. They protect your ego instead of fueling your growth. And you lose the quiet stars, the brilliant, unpolished voices who once believed you might hear them.

But you can choose differently. You can wake up tomorrow and stop performing competence. You can start cultivating it, with humility, with curiosity, and with a willingness to say:

"I don't know. But I want to learn."

"I got here one way. I want to grow another."

"I will not lead to preserve my image. I will lead to build something meaningful."

You can choose to lead not as the hero, but as the student. Not as the savior, but as the servant. Not because the job demands it, but because of the moment that does. And that moment begins when you stop defending your image and start discovering your impact.

This message isn't just for those with titles. It's for everyone who's been part of the system, everyone who's witnessed, endured, or even benefited from it. Maybe you learned to stay quiet. Maybe you used the system. Maybe you stopped asking whether the game itself was worth playing.

This is not a call for disruption for the sake of it. It's a quieter revolution. A revolution of soul. A refusal to trade integrity for access. A reminder that your loyalty should be to your principles. Your loyalty should be to the version of yourself you want your children, your friends, and your colleagues to remember.

Your voice matters. Your standards matter. And your courage, especially when no one is watching, has a ripple effect far beyond what you'll ever see.

You may already be a leader. Not in title, but in the moments when someone watches how you respond and chooses to follow your example.

Expect more of your leaders. Don't feed their ego. Feed their curiosity. Offer questions instead of compliments. Truth instead of applause. And most importantly: believe. Believe that if you want something to change, you must start with yourself. Because revolutions that start outside of us tend to burn out. But revolutions that start inside us? They last.

One day, sooner than you think, you'll find yourself in a room where you are the most powerful person present. And in that moment, you'll remember this:

Power doesn't come from title or control. Power comes from trust.

It comes from the trust others have chosen to place in you. That trust is not yours by right. It's a gift, and your highest duty is to honor it. Not with performance, but with presence. Not with certainty, but with courage. Not with control, but with integrity.

Real power is not about being unchallenged. It's about being worthy of the challenge. Let's begin there. Let's lead as if trust, not power, is the only currency that truly matters. Because the most radical form of privilege is this: to be fully human in a system that teaches us to forget what that means. Let us not forget.

Let's start there, with truth, with honor, and with each other.

Final Words to the Reader:

If you've made it to the end of this book, it means something in these pages spoke to you. Maybe you felt seen. Maybe you felt challenged. Perhaps a part of you felt misunderstood or even attacked. Or maybe you're reading this because a difficult experience drove you to seek out answers or meaning. Whatever brought you here, I want to tell you this: You are not alone.

There are many of us, quietly sitting in boardrooms and open-plan offices, attending the town halls, following the strategy slides, nodding along while something deeper inside us wonders, Is this really it?

We are part of a system that, despite its best intentions, too often forgets the humans inside it. And now, technology is revealing our cracks at an unprecedented speed. The old ways are no longer just outdated; they're exposed.

But here's the hopeful part: Awareness is the beginning of change.

So, I invite you to do something simple but radical. Step in front of the mirror, not the one shaped by your mortgage, your bonus plan, or the roles you've learned to play. Strip those things away for just a moment and ask yourself: Am I the leader I wish I had? Am I the employee my leader deserves?

That's where real transformation begins, not in the next reorg, not in a new app or framework, but in the daily choices we make with our integrity, our actions, and our willingness to collaborate with others who are trying, just like us.

If we do that, quietly and consistently, then yes, the world of work, and the world beyond it, really can become something better.

With honesty and hope,
Giovi

Resources and Further Reading

This section gathers the thinkers, texts, and concepts that informed the ideas explored throughout this book. It's not an exhaustive bibliography, but rather a curated set of sources for readers who wish to go deeper into the human, cultural, and structural dynamics shaping modern organizations.

1. Peter, Laurence J., and Raymond Hull. The Peter Principle: Why Things Always Go Wrong. New York: William Morrow and Company, 1969.
. This seminal work coined the term "Peter Principle," offering a satirical but painfully accurate diagnosis of bureaucratic failure: that people in a hierarchy tend to rise until they reach a role they can no longer perform competently.

2. See reporting on the Evolve Bank & Trust cybersecurity incident and executive resignations: Jack Naglieri, The Evolve Bank & Trust Breach (Detection at Scale, July 2024), which summarizes how unauthorized activity affected Evolve's systems and data, alongside reporting on leadership changes following regulatory scrutiny and fintech partner instability. Available at: detectionatscale.com/p/evolve-bank-breach

3. For an authoritative account of the TSB Bank 2018 IT migration failure, see the UK Financial Conduct Authority's press release: "TSB fined £48m for operational resilience failings," December 2022. Available at: fca.org.uk/news/press-releases/tsb-fined-48m-operational-resilience-failings

4. See Punjab National Bank scam reporting on Wikipedia and Reuters ("Lapses at many levels led to huge PNB fraud"), available at reuters.com/article/world/exclusivelapsesatmanylevelsofbankledtohuge-pnbfraudinternalreportidUSKBN1JG008.

5. For context on Brazil's fintech and digital banking disruptions, see broader reporting on operational issues and cyber challenges affecting Brazilian financial technology infrastructure, including cyberattacks on service providers tied to PIX payment systems and sectorwide digital transformation pressures in the banking industry. Relevant reporting and analysis include cyber incident coverage and fintech sector reviews. Available at bankinfosecurity.com/hackers-grab-130m-using-brazils-real-time-payment-system-a-29352.

6. Graeber, David. Bullshit Jobs: A Theory. New York: Simon & Schuster, 2018. In this influential work, anthropologist David Graeber argues that a significant portion of modern jobs, particularly in bureaucratic and corporate contexts, exist primarily to give the appearance of productivity, rather than serving any meaningful function. His analysis offers a provocative lens for understanding dysfunction in large institutions and the emotional toll of work without purpose.

7. Ibn Khaldun (1332–1406), The Muqaddimah: An Introduction to History, originally written in 1377, presents his theory of asabiyyah (social cohesion), showing how strong group solidarity fuels the rise of new powers but erodes as wealth and comfort grow, contributing to internal decay and eventual collapse. According to scholarly summaries of The Muqaddimah, asabiyyah is strongest at the beginning of a civilization's life cycle and weakens over time as elites become detached from hardship and shared purpose, leading to the decline of dynasties and their replacement by others with stronger group cohesion.

8. Alcacer, Juan, Tarun Khanna, and Christine Snively. "The Rise and Fall of Nokia." Harvard Business School Case 714428, originally published January 2014 (revised June 2020). This indepth case study examines Nokia's strategic decisions, organizational structures, cultural dynamics, and the challenges it faced, including the integration of Nokia Siemens Networks, as it struggled to adapt to industry disruption and internal inertia. Available from Harvard Business School Publishing as a case study for executive and leadership education.

9. Marcus Aurelius (121–180 AD), Meditations, translated by Gregory Hays (Modern Library, 2002), a widely respected English edition of the Roman emperor's Stoic reflections on leadership, virtue, ethics, and selfgovernance. Marcus wrote Meditations as a series of personal notes practicing Stoic philosophy, yet its themes on ethical leadership and moral clarity remain deeply relevant today. Available from major book retailers.

You may already be a leader. Not in title, but in the moments when someone watches how you respond and chooses to follow your example.